# English Grammar Exercises: A Complete Guide to English Tenses for ESL Students

## By Miles J̶

Copy̶ ̶ski 2013

The author asserts ̶ ̶moral right to be identified as the author of this work.

All rights reserved. No part of this book may be reproduced or transmitted in any form or by any means, electronic, mechanical, photocopying or otherwise, without the prior written permission of the author.

## Other Books by this Author

102 ESL Games and Activities for New and Prospective Teachers

102 ESL Games and Activities for Kids

Basic English Grammar: A Guide for New and Prospective ESL Teachers

# Table of Contents

Introduction..................................................................................7

The Present Simple: Structure and Use...........................................8

    The Present Simple: Exercise 1..............................................10

    The Present Simple: Exercise 2..............................................11

    The Present Simple: Exercise 3..............................................12

The Present Continuous: Structure and Use..................................13

    The Present Continuous: Exercise 1........................................14

    The Present Continuous: Exercise 2........................................15

    The Present Continuous: Exercise 3........................................16

The Present Continuous vs. the Present Simple............................17

    The Present Continuous vs. the Present Simple: Exercise 1.....18

    The Present Continuous vs. the Present Simple: Exercise 2.....19

    The Present Continuous vs. the Present Simple: Exercise 3.....20

The Past Simple Tense: Structure and Use....................................21

    The Past Simple: Exercise 1...................................................23

    The Past Simple: Exercise 2...................................................24

    The Past Simple: Exercise 3...................................................25

The Present Perfect: Structure and Use.........................................26

    The Present Perfect: Exercise 1..............................................28

The Present Perfect: Exercise 2..................................................29

The Present Perfect: Exercise 3..................................................30

The Present Perfect vs. the Past simple..........................................31

The Present Perfect vs. the Past Simple: Exercise 1..................32

The Present Perfect vs. the Past Simple: Exercise 2..................33

The Present Perfect vs. the Past Simple: Exercise 3..................34

The Past Continuous: Structure and Use........................................35

The Past Continuous: Exercise 1..............................................37

The Past Continuous: Exercise 2..............................................38

The Past Continuous: Exercise 3..............................................39

The Present Perfect Continuous: Structure and Use......................40

The Present Perfect Continuous: Exercise 1..............................42

The Present Perfect Continuous: Exercise 2..............................43

The Present Perfect Continuous: Exercise 3..............................44

The Past Perfect: Structure and Use..............................................45

The Past Perfect: Exercise 1....................................................46

The Past Perfect: Exercise 2....................................................47

The Past Perfect: Exercise 3....................................................48

The Past Perfect Continuous: Structure and Use............................49

Past Perfect Continuous: Exercise 1..........................................50

Past Perfect Continuous: Exercise 2..........................................51

Past Perfect Continuous: Exercise 3..........52
The Future simple: Structure and Use..........53
  The Future Simple: Exercise 1..........54
  The Future Simple: Exercise 2..........55
  The Future Simple: Exercise 3..........56
The Future Continuous: Structure and Use..........57
  The Future Continuous: Exercise 1..........58
  The Future Continuous: Exercise 2..........59
  The Future Continuous: Exercise 3..........60
The Future Perfect: Structure and Use..........61
  The Future Perfect: Exercise 1..........62
  The Future Perfect: Exercise 2..........63
  The Future Perfect: Exercise 3..........64
The Future Perfect Continuous: Structure and Use..........65
  The Future Perfect Continuous: Exercise 1..........66
  The Future Perfect Continuous: Exercise 2..........67
  The Future Perfect Continuous: Exercise 3..........68
Answer Key..........69
  The Present Simple: Exercise 1..........69
  The Present Simple: Exercise 2..........69
  The Present Simple: Exercise 3..........70

The Present Continuous: Exercise 1 ........................................... 71

The Present Continuous: Exercise 2 ........................................... 71

The Present Continuous: Exercise 3 ........................................... 72

The Present Continuous vs. the Present Simple: Exercise 1 ..... 73

The Present Continuous vs. the Present Simple: Exercise 2 ..... 73

The Present Continuous vs. the Present Simple: Exercise 3 ..... 74

The Past Simple: Exercise 1 ....................................................... 75

The Past Simple: Exercise 2 ....................................................... 75

The Past Simple: Exercise 3 ....................................................... 76

The Present Perfect: Exercise 1 .................................................. 77

The Present Perfect: Exercise 2 .................................................. 77

The Present Perfect: Exercise 3 .................................................. 78

The Present Perfect vs. the Past Simple: Exercise 1 .................. 79

The Present Perfect vs. the Past Simple: Exercise 2 .................. 79

The Present Perfect vs. the Past Simple: Exercise 3 .................. 80

The Past Continuous: Exercise 1 ............................................... 81

The Past Continuous: Exercise 2 ............................................... 81

The Past Continuous: Exercise 3 ............................................... 82

The Present Perfect Continuous: Exercise 1 .............................. 83

The Present Perfect Continuous: Exercise 2 .............................. 83

The Present Perfect Continuous: Exercise 3 .............................. 84

The Past Perfect: Exercise 1 .................................................. 85

The Past Perfect: Exercise 2 .................................................. 85

The Past Perfect: Exercise 3 .................................................. 86

The Past Perfect Continuous: Exercise 1 ............................... 87

The Past Perfect Continuous: Exercise 2 ............................... 87

The Past Perfect Continuous: Exercise 3 ............................... 88

The Future Simple: Exercise 1 ............................................... 89

The Future Simple: Exercise 2 ............................................... 89

The Future Simple: Exercise 3 ............................................... 90

The Future Continuous: Exercise 1 ........................................ 91

The Future Continuous: Exercise 2 ........................................ 91

The Future Continuous: Exercise 3 ........................................ 92

The Future Perfect: Exercise 1 ............................................... 93

The Future Perfect: Exercise 2 ............................................... 93

The Future Perfect: Exercise 3 ............................................... 94

The Future Perfect Continuous: Exercise 1 ........................... 95

The Future Perfect Continuous: Exercise 2 ........................... 95

The Future Perfect Continuous: Exercise 3 ........................... 96

Appendix 1 .............................................................................. 97

Appendix 2 .............................................................................. 98

Appendix 3 .............................................................................. 99

# Introduction

Congratulations on choosing this book, English Grammar Exercises: A Complete Guide to English Tenses for ESL Students. Learning to use English tenses correctly is very important to learning the English language. Once you understand the most common tenses, you'll find that the rest of the English language becomes so much easier! Don't worry; it's really not that hard!

This book will guide you through all of the tenses with clear explanations and exercises for each tense.

Read the Structure and Use section for each tense before you try the exercises. Then, complete the exercises; I recommend that you complete the exercises on a separate piece of paper, rather than in the book. This way, you are able to do the exercises again at a later date if you choose. You'll find, as you work through the different exercises, you gradually become more comfortable and confident in your English ability.

Spend the rest of your time trying to find examples of the tense you have just studied, in English books, films, songs and so on. Then practice making sentences of your own. When you feel ready, move onto the next tense.

After two, three or four weeks, you should understand the most important part of the English language: the tenses. Good luck!

# The Present Simple: Structure and Use

**Structure:** subject + base verb

**Examples:** "I like coffee." "They love football."

When the subject is "he," "she" or "it," we add "s" / "es" / "ies" to the verb in affirmative sentences. (Please see Appendix 1 for "s" / "es" / "ies" spelling rules)

**Examples:** "He takes a bus to work." "The kite flies very high in strong wind."

We form questions with "do" / "does" when the sentence doesn't contain the verb, "to be," and negatives with "don't" / "doesn't."

**I you we they:** do / don't

**Examples:** "Do you drink wine?" "I don't sleep early."

**He / she / it:** does / doesn't

**Examples:** "Does Alice study?" "He doesn't like sport."

When the sentence contains the verb "to be" we invert the subject and the verb to form questions. And add "not" to make negatives.

**I:** am (not)

**Examples:** "I'm a man." "I'm not a machine!"

**You / we / they:** are (not)

**Examples:** "Are you happy?" "John and I aren't thirsty."

**He she it: is (not)**

**Examples:** "Is Sally a teacher?" "That car isn't cheap."

We use the present simple to talk about habitual actions. That is, things that happen routinely or over and over again. For example, "I get up early in the morning." This means I get up early in the morning as a habit, or it is normal for me to get up early. I probably got up early yesterday, got up early today and will probably get up early tomorrow. Or, "Susan doesn't eat much for lunch." This means that everyday (or almost everyday) Susan eats very little for her lunch.

We also use the present simple to talk about facts or truths. For example, "Paris is the capital of France," "Sam drinks too much" or "Gerald loves riding his bicycle."

# The Present Simple: Exercise 1

Complete the following present simple sentences using one of the verbs below (remember that you may have to add s/es to the verb.) The first one has been done for you.

**Verbs: eat(s) read(s) go(es) x2 annoy(s) collect(s) bite(s) love(s) study(ies) hate (s)**

1. Mike <u>reads</u> a lot of books.

2. I _____ my son from school at 2:00pm

3. Claire _____ Mark.

4. Dave and Susana often _____ for a picnic in the park on weekends.

5. We _____ shopping at the weekend.

6. You really _____ me! Go away!

7. Be careful. That dog _____.

8. He _____ sociology at University.

9. Our son _____ to school every weekday.

10. Steven _____ spiders. They scare him!

# The Present Simple: Exercise 2

Complete the following present simple sentences using the words in the brackets and a form of "do." The first one has been done for you.

1. What time <u>do you get up</u>? (you / get up)

2. When _____ get home? (Maria / get home)

3. They _____ vegetables. (not / like)

4. Where _____ school? (they / attend)

5. _____ watching TV? (John / like)

6. Why _____ him so much? (you / like)

7. The sun _____ until 8:00. (not / rise)

8. _____ the same train every day? (they / take)

9. Why _____? It's bad for him. (he / smoke)

10. Americans _____ much tea. (not / drink)

# The Present Simple: Exercise 3

Complete the sentences using the correct form of the verbs below. The sentences may be affirmative, questions or negatives so you may need to use do / does. The first one has been done for you.

**Verbs: take eat cost (x2) be live come exercise from go(x2)**

1. Anacondas eat meat

2. I live in America. Where ___ you ___?

3. It _____ me 1 hour to get to work.

4. Argentineans _____ from Brazil.

5. The capital of Spain ____ Madrid.

6. It looks nice. How much ___ it ___?

7. I don't want it. It _____ too much.

8. The earth _____ around the sun.

9. The sun _____ around the earth.

10. You are very healthy. ____ you _____ everyday?

# The Present Continuous: Structure and Use

**Structure:** Subject + present form of verb "to be" + present participle (Please see Appendix 2 for present participle spelling rules)

**Examples:** "She is cooking," "I'm writing" "They are playing football."

We form questions by inverting the subject and verb "to be" and negatives by adding "not" to the verb "to be."

**Examples:** "Is he reading?" "We aren't singing."

We use the present continuous to talk about things that are happening now. For example, "I am writing" or "You are reading." We also use the present continuous to talk about future arrangements. When we do this we usually include a time, a date or some other time reference. For example, "I'm meeting my wife later," "He is playing tennis tonight" or "We are going to Mexico in August."

In addition we can use the present continuous to talk about things happening *around now*. For example, "I'm studying philosophy at Uni." In fact, I'm not studying this very second, but I am attending a three year course. Or, "I'm drinking a lot of tea these days." Again, not this very second, I'm actually drinking a beer, but generally these days I'm drinking a lot of tea, more tea than usual.

# The Present Continuous: Exercise 1

Complete the following present continuous sentences using one of the verbs below and a form of the verb "to be." The first one has been done for you.

**play bark do meet have (x2) try watch study work**

1. A: What're you doing? B: Nothing, really. I'<u>m watching</u> TV.

2. A: Are you busy? B: A little, I _____ my homework.

3. A: Where's Tony? B: Oh, he _____ football this evening.

4. Please don't disturb me. I_____ to get some work done.

5. A: Why do you look so tired? B: Oh, because I_____ nights at the moment.

6. A: What are Dave and Aaron doing later tonight? B: They _____ friends at the cinema.

7. A: Is Mezut here? B: No, he_____ in the library.

8. A: How's Jane? B: Not so good. She_____ problems with Jack, her boyfriend.

9. A: What's for dinner? B: We _____ steak and potatoes.

10. The neighbour's dog_____ a lot, isn't it?

# The Present Continuous: Exercise 2

Complete these present continuous sentences using the words in brackets and a form of the verb "to be". The first one has been done for you.

1. What're you doing tonight? (you / do)

2. I _____ to sleep late tonight. (not / go)

3. _____ to visit us tonight? (they / come)

4. What _____ over Christmas? (you / do)

5. _____ all the hot water again? (he / use)

6. They _____ . They're drowning! (not / swim)

7. Kieron _____ very well at school at the moment (not / do)

8. Thomas _____. He's staying at home. (not / work)

9. We _____ on holiday this summer (not / go)

10. It _____ well. I think it might be broken. (not / work)

# The Present Continuous: Exercise 3

Complete the following present continuous sentences using one of the verbs below and a form of the verb "to be." The sentences may be affirmative, questions or negatives. The first one has been done for you.

**drink decorate sleep move go eat cycle swim hide work**

1. I'm not swimming today. It's too cold.

2. I'm a bit worried about Theo. He ………. too much beer.

3. You look nice! _____ out?

4. What _____, Susan? It looks delicious.

5. I _____! I'm just resting my eyes.

6. Kate _____ to work today. I hope she doesn't get too tired.

7. We _____ the front room. It'll be too expensive.

8. I can't see you! _____ somewhere?

9. Terry and June are spending the day in the garden. They_____ today.

10. I saw a "For Sale" sign on your house! _____?

# The Present Continuous vs. the Present Simple

Choosing between the two tenses can often be difficult. Remember, we use the present simple for facts or truths and things that happen over and over again, habitual actions. For example, "The earth is round (ish)," "The sun is hot," "I drink coffee in the morning" or "I run 6 miles every evening."

We use the present continuous for things happening now; they haven't finished. For example, "I'm writing." In addition we can use the present continuous for arrangements, "I'm meeting John at 6:00."

Moreover, we often use the present continuous for temporary states and the present simple for more permanent states. For example, "I'm working at the mall" vs "I work at the mall." In the first example I consider it a temporary job and will probably find another job soon. In the second example I consider it permanent. I imagine myself working there in the future and have no plans to change job.

There are also several words that we do not commonly use in the continuous tense. The most common of these are: "love" "hate" "like" "need" "want" "prefer" "believe" "know" "remember" "understand" "belong" "seem" "smell" "hear" "sound" "see" "taste" "agree" "surprise" "be" "cost" and "owe."

So, "I'm hungry. I want some food" not, "I'm wanting some food" and "I understand" not, "I'm understanding."

# The Present Continuous vs. the Present Simple: Exercise 1

Which is the correct verb form? The first one has been done for you

1. I can't help you at the moment. *I'm watching* / *I watch* the football.

2. What *are you doing* / *do you do* this weekend?

3. Water *is boiling* / *boils* at 100 degrees Celsius.

4. *I'm not working* / *I don't work* this Friday

5. Are Susan and James here? No, they *are playing* / *play* outside.

6. I'm really thirsty. *I'm wanting* / *I want* a drink.

7. *Do you understand?* / *Are you understanding*?

8. I find it difficult to wake up in the morning. I *always drink* / *am always drinking* lots of coffee.

9. *I don't like* / *I'm not liking* this movie.

10. *I sleep in* / *I'm sleeping in* on weekends

# The Present Continuous vs. the Present Simple: Exercise 2

Complete the following sentences by put the verb in either the present simple or present continuous tense. The first one has been done for you.

1. Where's Nicholas? Oh, in his room. He is reading. (read)

2. I'm a vegetarian. I _____ meat (not / eat)

3. Oh wow! Dinner _____ delicious. (smell)

4. I've got a lot of work to do before Friday so I _____ quite hard. (work)

5. I _____ alcohol. It gives me a headache. (not / drink)

6. I'm exhausted. I _____ to bed. (go)

7. I'm a truck driver. I _____ trucks for a living. (drive)

8. We _____ to Brazil for our holidays this year. (go)

9. He _____ us for dinner. He says he isn't hungry. (not / join)

10. I _____ in magic. (not / believe)

# The Present Continuous vs. the Present Simple: Exercise 3

Complete the sentences using one of the verbs below in the present simple or the present continuous. The sentences may be positive, negative or questions. The first one has been done for you.

**live read taste chase come drip cost go happens damages**

1. Smoking *damages* your health.

2. I _____ much. I just don't have the time.

3. ____ this milk _____ funny to you?

4. Penguins _____ from the South Pole.

5. What's all that noise outside? What _____?

6. No, I'm not going to buy this coat. It _____ too much.

7. Komodo dragons _____ on the island of Komodo, in Indonesia.

8. Cats _____ dogs.

9. It's so hot! I _____ with sweat

10. ___ you ____ out this weekend?

# The Past Simple Tense: Structure and Use

**Structure:** subject + past verb

**Examples:** "I saw a good movie last week." "I ate breakfast at 8:00 in the morning."

We form questions and negatives with did / didn't when the sentence does not contain "was" / "were."

**Examples:** "Did they win the game?" "We didn't see any clouds."

When the sentence contains "was" / "were" we invert the subject and the verb to form questions and add "not" to make negatives.

**You / we / they: were (not)**

**Examples:** "Were Rachel and Tina at the park last night?" "We weren't happy yesterday."

**I / he / she / it: was (not)**

**Examples:** "Was Theo in the team?" "I wasn't happy."

We use the past simple tense to talk about things that started and finished at a specific time in the past. For example, "I went to the mall yesterday" or "I broke my leg when I was six."

We also commonly use the past simple to tell a narrative, or story. For example, "Yesterday I got up and had breakfast. But I felt tired so I went back to bed. Then…." And so on. It is common to use sequencing words such as, "first," "after that," and "finally" with the past simple.

We form regular past verbs by adding "ed" to the base form of the verb. For example, "work" to "worked" or "jump" to "jumped." However, many verbs in English are irregular and, unfortunately, the irregular verbs are some of our most common. (Please see Appendix 3 for a list of our most common irregular verbs.)

# The Past Simple: Exercise 1

Put the verb in brackets into its past form in order to complete the following past simple sentences. The first one has been done for you.

1. I <u>walked</u> to work. (walk)

2. He _____ tired. ( be)

3. Kate _____ him. (love)

4. We _____ the children from school. (collect)

5. They _____ a fish. (catch)

6. We _____ the football match. (watch)

7. Giroud _____ a goal! (score)

8. Pluto the dog _____ all his food. (eat)

9. Tom _____ at home all day. (stay)

10. John and his wife _____ in yesterday morning. (sleep)

# The Past Simple: Exercise 2

Complete the following past simple sentences using the words in the brackets. The sentences may be positive negative or affirmative. The first one has been done for you.

1. It was raining yesterday and I didn't want to get wet so <u>I didn't go</u> out. (I / go)

2. A: What _____ yesterday? (you / do) B: Oh nothing. _____ in. (I stay)

3. A: I think we have a test today. B: How do you know? _____ the teacher (you ask) because _____ me. (nobody / tell)

4. A: I can't find my pen. _____ it without asking again? (you/ borrow) Bb: No, where _____ it. (you leave)

5. I don't think John and Kate know about the meeting. _____ it this morning. (John / mention)

6. A: It's hot isn't it. I hope _____ to pack the sun shade. (you / remember) B: Oh course I did. _____ it.(I / forget)

7.. Thanks for letting me borrow you laptop yesterday, but I'm afraid _____! (it / break)

8. Sorry _____ the dishes. I was just so busy! (I / do)

9. _____ James and Lisa yesterday. (I / see) _____well, really healthy.(they / look)

10. Did _____ you about their trip? (they / tell) _____ fantastic! (it / sound)

# The Past Simple: Exercise 3

Complete the sentences using the correct form of the verbs below. The sentences may be affirmative, questions or negatives. The first one has been done for you.

**break be (x3) go (x2) pass use enjoy fall have see say sleep seem do could happen**

1. What a night! I <u>didn't go</u> to bed until half twelve in the morning. We're crazy!

2. I _____ to Spain last year. I _____ it a lot. It _____ really interesting.

3. Sorry! I think I _____ all the hot water.

4. That match _____ incredible! I _____ believe my eyes!

5. We _____ very well last night. It _____ so noisy!

6. What _____ Mike _____ to you? He _____ angry.

7. Well, the court has found me guilty, but I swear I _____ it.

8. Hurrah. I _____ my driving test yesterday!

9. ___ you _____ that movie yesterday? It _____ Tom Cruise in it. I like him.

10. What happened to your arm? I _____ out of a tree and _____ it.

# The Present Perfect: Structure and Use

**Structure:** Subject + have / has + past participle

**I you we they: have**

**Examples:** "I have been to India" "We have lived in Spain for 6 years."

**He she it: has**

**Examples:** "He has eaten the biscuits" "She has caught the train."

We form questions by inverting the subject and "have" / "has" and form negatives by adding, "not" to "have" / "has"

**Examples:** "Has he shut the door?" "Have they gone on holiday?" "She hasn't seen my keys" "You haven't finished your homework."

We form the past participle by adding "ed" to regular verbs. (For some of our common irregular verbs please see [Appendix 3](#).)

We use the present perfect tense in three ways.

1. To talk about experiences that happened at an unspecified point in the past; it's not important or stated when the experience occurred. For example, "I've been to Spain" ("when" isn't important but at some point in the past I went to Spain) or "She has tried snake meat" (Again, we don't care when but she has, at some point in her life, tasted snake meat.)

2. To talk about something that happened in the past that has a present result. For example, "I've cleaned the house" (I cleaned the house in the past and the house is clean now) or "I've drunk all

the milk in the fridge" (at some point in the past I drank all the milk in the fridge and the result is that now there is no milk in the fridge!)

3. To talk about a state or action that began in the past and continues up to now. For example, "I've been scared of snake for 5 years" (Five years ago I began to be scared of snakes, I continued to be scared of snake for the next five years and now I am still scared of snakes) or "I've lived in London for 6 years" (I moved to London 6 years ago, stayed there for the next 6 years and now I still live in London.) We commonly use for / since when using this aspect of the present perfect. Use "for" for periods of time such as 6 years or 2 days, and "since" for points of time such as, "since 1980" and "since Tuesday."

# The Present Perfect: Exercise 1

Complete the present perfect sentences below using the verbs in brackets. The first one has been done for you.

1. I <u>have been</u> to the shops to buy some food. (be)

2. He _____ at the company for two years. He likes it there. (work)

3. Another rainy day. We _____ the sun for weeks. (not see)

4. I _____ my bag! It was under the sofa. (find)

5. _____ you _____ John? (meet) He's my brother.

6. Maria _____ (not read) it. I keep telling her to but she never gets around to it.

7. Mark _____ (have) seven different jobs in the last year. I wish he didn't get fired all the time!

8. They _____ (not buy) a car yet, so we'll have to give them a lift.

9. My computer _____ (break) again. I really need a new one.

10. No, I _____ (not see) her all week. Maybe she's ill?

# The Present Perfect: Exercise 2

Complete the following present perfect sentences using one of the verbs below. The sentences may be affirmative, questions or negatives. The first one has been done for you.

**go be x3 finished get eat paint invite finish**

1. I've eaten too much. I think I need a nap.

2. ___ Steven ____ the living room yet? I want it to look nice for Christmas.

3. ____ you ____ with the scissors. I need them.

4. Where ____ the cat _____. I can't find it.

5. I _____ to Zurich. I'd love to go!

6. The dog _____ bad, so I've locked it outside.

7 _____ you _____ dinner yet? I want to wash up.

8. Mike and June _____ us for dinner tonight.

9. ____ we ___ any wine? We need something to drink with dinner.

10. I _____ a teacher for over a decade.

# The Present Perfect: Exercise 3

Complete the following sentences with "for" / "since." The first one has been done for you.

1. He has lived here <u>for</u> 6 years.

2. I have walked _____ 6:00 a.m. to get here.

3. We've had this car _____ 15 years.

4. I've been here _____ this morning.

5. I've loved pizza _____ I was a little boy.

6. It feels like I've been a father ___ ages.

7. She's smoked _____ she started University.

8. I've studied Philosophy _____ a decade

9. They've been married _____ 1991.

10. I've drunk four coffees ____ this morning.

# The Present Perfect vs. the Past simple

These two tenses are often used incorrectly by non-native speakers of English. Remember that the past simple refers to a specific point in the past. So, "I went to Spain last year." "Last year" is a specific time in the past and this is why we use the past simple. Compare this to "I've been to Spain." Here we have no specific time reference and are simply saying, "at some point in the past," and so we use the present perfect. In addition, we use the past simple to refer to an action that is finished / completed / over and has no connection to the present while we can use the present perfect to refer to something with a present result. Compare "I lost my key last week" to "I've lost my key." The first sentence, in the past simple, refers to a past action that has no connection to the present. In all probability the speaker found his key or had a new one made, but whether he did or not is unimportant, we only know that he lost his key. The second sentence however, in the present perfect, means that the speaker lost his key in the past and *his key is still lost*. Finally, if we are talking about a period of time that started in the past and continues to the present, then we use the present perfect, for example, "I've had a dog for 6 years."

# The Present Perfect vs. the Past Simple: Exercise 1

Are the following sentences grammatically correct, or incorrect? The first one has been done for you.

1. What time did he leave? <u>Correct</u>

2. He's returned home 4 hours ago._____

3. They've cooked dinner yesterday. _____

4. Well, he didn't call yet so we'll have to wait. _____

5. I'm looking for the Norris's. Have you seen them? _____

6. Did you live here all your life? _____

7. I've been quite ill this week. _____

8. She was quite ill last week. _____

9. Have you seen my purse? I've lost it. _____

10. Did you have fun at school today? _____

# The Present Perfect vs. the Past Simple: Exercise 2

Choose the correct tense from the following examples. The first one has been done for you.

1. I *went* / *have been* to Italy 2 years ago.

2. *Have you seen / Did you see* Marcus last week?

3. Quick, get help! *I broke / I've broken* my leg.

4. *I've lived / I lived* in this house for 15 years.

5. You look different. *Did you have / Have you had* your hair cut?

6. John just stole 40 dollars from my purse. Hmm, he *didn't change / hasn't changed*.

7. *Have you ever been / Did you ever go* to India?

8. Oh no! It's raining and *I forgot / I've forgotten* my umbrella.

9. I used to live in Thailand, and I could speak Thai. But *I forgot / I've forgotten* it all now.

10. Mozart *wrote / has written* The Magic Flute.

# The Present Perfect vs. the Past Simple: Exercise 3

Complete the following affirmative / interrogative sentences with one of the verbs below in the correct tense: past simple or present perfect. The first one has been done for you.

**Live lose move kill love get walk gain be (x2)**

1. They live in Boston, but they <u>lived</u> in New York for ten years.

2. Terry can't find her lap top. She _____ it.

3. Einstein _____ a very intelligent man.

4. The second world war _____ over 50 million people.

5. I _____ to play soccer when I was younger.

6. When ___ you _____ your new job. It sounds amazing!

7. How ___ you _____. I've missed you!

8. When _____ you and Sam ___ here?

9. _____ you _____ the dog yet?

10. India _____ independence in 1947.

# The Past Continuous: Structure and Use

**Structure:** Subject + was / were + present participle

**I he she it: was**

**You we they: were**

**Examples:** "He was running" "They were watching TV"

We form questions by inverting the subject and the verb and negatives by adding "not" to the verb, "to be"

**Examples:** "Were you swimming?" "I wasn't looking."

The past continuous emphasises continuous actions (actions that continue for a period of time) and we use it in three main ways:

1. To talk about an action that was happening both before and after a specific point in the past. For example, "At 12:00 p.m. yesterday she was cooking lunch." (Before 12:00 pm she was cooking lunch, at 12:00 pm she was cooking lunch and after 12:00pm she was cooking lunch. In other words, at 12:00 pm she was in the middle of cooking lunch!)

2. To begin, and help tell, a story. Stories are told mostly in the past simple and the past continuous helps to give back ground information or set the scene.  For example, "It was raining hard and I was reading a book by the fire. Suddenly, the phone rang. It was John with some bad news. I ran to the car…" and so on. Or, "Tony and Susan were walking by the edge of the river when Susan slipped! She fell right into the river so Tony dived in after her…"

3. To talk about two or more actions that are happening at the same time in the past. For example, "I was doing my homework while Mum was working on the computer and Dad was doing the dishes." Or, "We were playing football in the park. It was raining and we were getting cold."

# The Past Continuous: Exercise 1

Complete the following past continuous sentences using the verbs below. The first one has been done for you.

**sing read clean wear feel (x2) come think drink cook**

1. When the phone rang I <u>was reading</u> a magazine

2. They _____ tea and eating cake when we arrived.

3. _____ the children _____ up the sitting room? They have to before our guests arrive.

4. They _____ their coats. No wonder they caught colds.

5. What _____ Ozil _____? He was helping Geroud.

6. _____ Wilbur and Alistair _____ ok? I know they were ill.

7. I _____ about going back to University but changed my mind.

8. He _____ when I arrived so I knew it would be a while before we ate.

9. John _____ in the shower. It sounded really nice.

10. We _____ great. It had been a long, tiring 33 hour trip.

# The Past Continuous: Exercise 2

Complete the following sentences in either the past continuous or the past simple using the verbs in brackets. The first one has been done for you.

1. I <u>was walking</u> (walk) to work when I had (have) a great idea!

2. ____you____(see) the match last night? I____(watch) it at Terry's house.

3. It was a bit of a surprise to see Ann yesterday. We _____ (argue) about something when she _____!(arrive)

4. Why ___you _____ (crash) the car? ___you____(talk) on the phone again?

5. _____ Dave ____(let) the dog out? I think he _____ (need) some fresh air.

6. When I was younger we ____(live) in Brazil for a year.

7. I ____(go) to bed early last night.

8. Dad _____(play) computer games when I _____ (go) to bed.

9. I _____ an old student yesterday.(met) She _____(shop) for Christmas presents.

10. John Lennon _____ (write) some great songs. It's a shame he ____(die) so young.

# The Past Continuous: Exercise 3

Complete the following sentences in the past continuous or past simple using the verbs below. The first one has been done for you.

**argue walk go catch drink sleep (x2) talk see try have**

1. I <u>was walking</u> to work at 8:00 am yesterday.

2. I _____ to my boss before starting the new project.

3. He _____ the ball twice during the game.

4. After lunch I _____ home.

5. I feel terrible! I _____ too much wine last night.

6. I _____ when the alarm clock rang.

7. Sorry I'm late. I _____ in.

8. I _____ a bath when you texted me.

9. I ___ Dave queuing outside the theatre yesterday. He _____ to get tickets for that new play.

10. I quickly left the room because they _____.

# The Present Perfect Continuous: Structure and Use

**Structure:** Subject + have / has + been + present participle

**I you we they: have**

Examples: "We've been thinking about you" "You have been sleeping."

**He she it: has**

Examples: "She's been working hard" "He's been losing weight."

We form questions by inverting the subject and "have" / "has" and form negatives by adding "not" to "have" / "has."

**Examples:** "Have you been working hard?" "Has she been reading?" "We haven't been sleeping" "He hasn't been cooking."


The present perfect continuous emphasises the continuous aspect of an action that began in the past and continues up to the present (and possibly into the future.) We use this tense in two main ways.

1. To talk about an action that started at some point in the past, continues up to the present and may (or may not) continue into the future. It is very common to use "for" and "since" with this use of the present continuous. For example, "I've been learning English for 6 years." So, I started learning English 6 years ago, I'm leaning English now and maybe I will continue to learn English in the future (or maybe not, it's unimportant.) Or, for example, "They've been arguing since breakfast time." So, they started arguing at breakfast, are still arguing now and *may* argue into the future.

This meaning is very similar to the present perfect simple, and often identical. We use the continuous form either because we view it as a continuous action or because we view it as more temporary.

2. To talk about an action that started in the past and has just / recently finished. For example, "I've been eating the cake" (I have now stopped. Maybe I got full.) Or, "They've been cleaning the room" (Again, they have now stopped. Maybe they got tired or bored of cleaning.)

Again, we are interested in the continuous action, but this time if we compare it to the present perfect the differences are greater. If we put the two examples above into the present simple tense, we get a very different meaning as we are more concerned with results rather than the action. For example, "I have eaten the cake" means that the cake is finished and, "They've cleaned the room" means that the room is now clean.

# The Present Perfect Continuous: Exercise 1

Complete the following present perfect continuous sentences using the verbs below. The first one has been done for you.

**Smoke drive do (x2) cook live use think work wait**

1. What's that lovely smell? <u>Have you been cooking</u>?

2. How long ___you_____here? It seems like a nice town.

3. I _____ since I was 15. I should really stop.

4. She _____ for a long time. I think she should pull over and take a break.

5. You're really wet! What _____you_____?

6. We _____ all day. We're really tired.

7. What ___ the dog _____? He looks really guilty.

8. That's a big water bill. _____we really _____so much water?

9. I _____about getting a new job. I'm not enjoying this one anymore.

10. Great, the new album is out. I _____for it for so long!

# The Present Perfect Continuous: Exercise 2

Choose the correct tense: present perfect or present perfect continuous. The first one has been done for you.

1. How long have you *been having / had* a dog?

2. You look tired. Have you *run / been running*?

3. Ah, good. I feel better now that I have *eaten / been eating*.

4. You smell. Have you *smoked / been smoking* again?

5. I'm exhausted. I've *worked / been working* for 14 days straight!

6. I've *thought / been thinking* about going away this weekend. What do you think?

7. They've *eaten / been eating* all the ice cream!

8. They haven't *seen / been seeing* the movie yet.

9. We've *played / been playing* football in the park. That's why we are so dirty.

10. John's *caught / been catching* a huge fish! We're having it for dinner!

# The Present Perfect Continuous: Exercise 3

Complete the following sentences using the verbs below in the present perfect or present perfect continuous. The first one has been done for you.

**eat do (x2) finish drink learn run put plan turn**

1. Have you <u>eaten</u> yet? I'm starving.

2. How's Dave _____ at school. He's just started his final year, hasn't he?

3. Where have you _____ the corkscrew? I can't find it.

4. I haven't _____ for ages. I might do a few miles tonight.

5. Alice and Tarquin have _____ their wedding for ages. I hope it goes well.

6. Hi Michelle! I haven't seen you for ages. What have you _____?

7. Has Rupam _____ his homework yet?

8. Where's Kate _____ Chinese? I might go along with her one day before my big trip.

9. No, sorry, I can't drive. I've _____.

10. There's something wrong with the electricity. The lights have _____ on and off all day.

# The Past Perfect: Structure and Use

**Structure:** Subject + had + past participle

**Examples:** "I'd seen the movie before" "We'd found 6 dollars behind the couch."

We form questions by inverting the subject and "had" and negatives by adding "not" to "had."

**Examples:** "Had you finished?" "I hadn't caught a cold."

We use the past perfect, very frequently in conjunction with the past simple tense, to talk about a state that existed or action that occurred *before another point in the past*. So, for example, "When I got home, they had eaten dinner." The first action is them eating dinner and the second, me getting home. Or, "She'd finished all the housework by the time he arrived." The first action is her finishing the house work and the second is him arriving. The first state or action / state will always be in the past perfect wherever it is placed in the sentence. One last example, "She was happy to see him as he'd lived in a different country for so long." Of course, the first action / state is him living in a different country and the second, her being happy to see him.

Contrast this to the past simple which we use in for simple narratives: first, then, after that and so on.

# The Past Perfect: Exercise 1

Complete the following past perfect sentences using the words in brackets. The first one has been done for you.

1. I <u>had</u> never <u>been</u> to Italy before so I really enjoyed it. (be)

2. She _____ her key by the time we got home. (find)

3. We _____ lost but Michael found us eventually. (get)

4. We saw a beautiful bird but it _____ its wing (hurt)

5. She went home but she _____ that she was supposed to work late. (forget)

6. How long ___ you ___ in England before Mark was born? (live)

7. When he met Suzanna, he _____ single for 6 years. (be)

8. We _____ by the time he woke up. (leave)

9. Molly and I _____ for 8 hours. We were starving. (eat)

10. When you met Gary, ____ you _____ your haircut? (have)

# The Past Perfect: Exercise 2

Complete the following past perfect sentences with one of the words below. The first one has been done for you.

**lose complete see stay buy leave bring repaired take think**

1. By the time the match started he_'d completed his_ homework.

2. ____ they _____ the movie you rented for them?

3. We _____ we'd need to bring any money so we had to go back and get some.

4. We weren't tired but he _____ up all last night so he had to go to bed early.

5. His phone broke but he couldn't return it as he _____ the receipt.

6. Alice _____ lots of text books but unfortunately, not the one we needed.

7. ____ they _____ the car when you got to the garage?

8. I got to the bar by 9:00 pm but they ___already _____.

9. They _____ her dress when I saw them in the mall. They said they could find the right size.

10. When I got home she _____ the dog for a walk. So I didn't need to go out again.

# The Past Perfect: Exercise 3

Choose the correct tense, past perfect or past simple. The first one has been done for you.

1. I felt a little sleepy so I *had taken / took* a nap.

2. I went to the bank and then I *had gone / went* to the post office.

3. The chicken looked lovely but it *hadn't been / wasn't* cooked properly. It was still raw!

4. She went to her yoga class but *had forgotten / forgot* her clothes so couldn't do it.

5. When they got to Thailand, they *had been / were* on a plane for 12 hours.

6. They watched the movie in French because they *had learnt / learned* French in high school.

7. Phillipe *had married / married* his high school sweetheart and they lived happily ever after.

8. We *had caught / caught* the 7:00 train and arrived at the station 6hrs later.

9. *Had you heard / Did you hear* that thunder last night?

10. After it stopped raining I *had gone / went* for a walk.

# The Past Perfect Continuous: Structure and Use

**Structure:** subject + had + been + present participle

**Examples:** "They had been walking for a long time" "She had been working."

We form questions by inverting the subject and "had" and negatives by adding "not" to "had."

**Examples:** "Had he been driving?" "I hadn't been thinking."

We use the present perfect continuous, like the past perfect, to talk about an action that started at some point in the past and continued to another point in the past. This second point will almost always be in the past simple. For example, "I'd been watching TV for 6 hours when I decided to turn it off" or "They'd been waiting a long time when I finally arrived." The past perfect continuous focuses heavily on the continuity of the action and its duration. Hence we frequently use it with "for" "since" and other time words. For example, "I'd been sleeping for 6 hours when she woke me," "We'd been doing the jigsaw since 6:00PM when we realised 2 pieces were missing" or "I'd been dreaming of travel all my life and one day I finally got the chance."

# Past Perfect Continuous: Exercise 1

Complete the following past perfect continuous sentences using the verbs below. The first one has been done for you.

**Live sail steal think paint take cook do (x2) walk**

1. I had been living in New York for 3 yrs when I met him.

2. He _____ portraits all his life but didn't recognize his own work.

3. She _____ since early morning and her feet were aching.

4. Did the police stop them because they _____?

5. They ____not_____ for a long time and enjoyed being on the ocean again.

6. I _____ of her when she phoned.

7. We _____ all morning, and the kitchen was a mess!

8. What ____you____ to make her so angry?

9. What exercise ____you_____ before your knee started hurting?

10. I _____ orders all morning from my boss and my head was hurting.

# Past Perfect Continuous: Exercise 2

Complete the following sentences using the verbs in brackets. One verb should be in the past perfect continuous, the other in the past simple. The first one has been done for you.

1. It was a beautiful day when they __got__ (get) to the beach. They <u>had been waiting</u> (wait) for this moment all week.

2. She _____ (see) him for over a year when he finally _____ her to marry him. (ask)

3. Before he _____ (move) to Spain, he _____ (live) at home in the U.S.

4. She _____ (wait) for this chance and _____ (take) it.

5. They _____ (could not) hear very well because they _____ (listen) to loud music.

6. Mary ____ (drink) coffee all morning and so _____ (start) to feel a bit light headed.

7. We _____ (shoot) the lion because it _____ (kill) villagers in the area.

8. Dinosaurs _____ (live) on the earth for millions of years before they _____ (become) extinct.

9. I _____ (jog) every other day and _____ (think) I was quite fit.

10. Mike _____ (want) to meet me at the airport, but he _____ (work) and was very tired.

# Past Perfect Continuous: Exercise 3

Complete the following sentences in either the past perfect continuous or past simple using the verbs below. The first one has been done for you.

**see rain meet clean be drive swim write work play**

1. It had been raining since I got up but I needed to leave the house.

2. She _____ her best friend on the way to work and stopped to talk.

3. I was so bored as I _____ the house all day.

4. Elvis _____ many of his own songs but he was very successful.

5. I looked at the clock. I _____ soccer for 6 hours.

6. Alexander _____ a great military leader and conquered much of the known world.

7. I needed to get to California by morning so I _____ for 14 hours.

8. I _____ most of the day so took a break.

9. When I got to the swimming pool Jack _____ for 2 hours.

10. They _____ a huge lion when they were on safari.

# The Future simple: Structure and Use

**Structure:** Subject + will + base form of the verb

**Examples:** "He'll be here this evening." "I'll put the kettle on"

We form questions by inverting the subject and "will" and form negatives by using "won't."

**Examples:** "Will he read his book?" "We won't stop working."

We use will for two main reasons.

1. To predict the future. For example, "Fearne will love University" or "Max will pass this exam easily."

Please note that we do not use, "will" for future plans. For future plans we instead use "going to." For example, "I'm going to study Sociology at University" or "I'm going to paint this room soon." For arrangements, as you looked at earlier, with a time or a date, we use the present continuous, for example, "She's leaving at 6:00 pm" or "They're walking to the lake after breakfast."

2. To make a quick / instant decision. For example, "Are you hungry? I'll make you a sandwich" or "It's a lovely day. I'll put on some shorts."

# The Future Simple: Exercise 1

Complete the following future simple sentences using one of the verbs below. The first one has been done for you.

**live run will melt be (x2) get meet beat ask do**

1. I don't think he'_ll be_ here by 6:00.

2. Is that the phone? I _____ it.

3. Man _____ on Mars in the future.

4. The icecaps _____ if we don't stop global warming.

5. Germany _____ England in the soccer match.

6. I _____ them if they need a lift.

7. I _____ it tomorrow.

8. We _____ out of money if we are not careful.

9. We'd better buy some wood. Winter this year _____ cold.

10. Ok then, we _____ you in the bar later.

# The Future Simple: Exercise 2

Choose the correct verb form, future simple or be going to. The first one has been done for you.

1. *Will you / <u>Are you going to</u>* go on holiday this year?

2. Scientist predict that the storm *will / is going to* be the worst for a decade.

3. A: Why did you buy all that paint? B: Oh, I *will / am going to* paint the bathroom.

4. A: I've lost my pen. B: Oh, don't worry. I *will / am going to* lend you mine.

5. A: Have you decided what to study at University? B: Yes, I *will / am going to* study computer science.

6. A: Did you forget the sandwiches? B: Oh no, yes I did. Never mind, we *will / are going to* buy some on the way.

7. Sorry, that's my other phone. I *will / am going to* ring you back.

8. I'm going out now. I might be a bit late. Maria *will / is going to* show me her holiday photos.

9. Well, what did he say? *Will he / Is he going to* get married?

10. A. I think the baby is crying again. B: Ok, I *will / am going to* get him.

# The Future Simple: Exercise 3

Complete the following future simple / be going to sentences using one of the verbs below. The first one has been done for you.

**be(x4) go make move arrive do (x2)**

1. I <u>am going to be</u> a doctor when I grow up.

2. A. I'm not sure how to turn the oven. B: Hang on I _____ it for you.

3. Where _____ you _____ on your holidays this summer?

4. Can you buy some flour and eggs? I _____ a cake this evening.

5. A: Did you finish your homework? B: No, I forgot. Thanks for reminding me. I _____ it now.

6. A: _____ you _____ to John's house later? B: No, he called earlier and cancelled.

7. I'm not sure about their car. It looks really old. Do you think it _____ ok?

8. Put on your coat! No? Ok, then…but you _____ cold.

9. A: What time will they arrive? B: Um, well, they left 2 hours ago, so they _____ here in about 20 minutes.

10. A: Are they really selling their house? B: Yes, I spoke to them yesterday. They _____ to Mississipi.

# The Future Continuous: Structure and Use

**Structure:** Subject + will + be + present participle

**Examples:** "They'll be swimming" "He'll be watching T.V."

We form questions by inverting the subject and "will" and negatives by replacing "will" with "won't."

**Examples:** "Will we be listening to music?" "They won't be going out later."

We use the future continuous to talk about an action(s) occurring at a specific time in the future. For example, "At 10 o'clock tonight, I'll be eating dinner" ("10 o'clock tonight" is obviously the specific time in the future. I will start eating some time before 10 o'clock and finish eating sometime after 10 o'clock) or "She'll be sleeping when we get there, so be quiet" (She will go to sleep before we arrive and continue to sleep after we have arrived.)

# The Future Continuous: Exercise 1

Complete the following future continuous sentences using one of the verbs below. The first one has been done for you.

**sleep work(x2) stay play meet arrive sell feel**

1. You should start the fire or we <u>will be feeling</u> cold tonight!

2. Don't wait for me to get back. I _____ out late tonight.

3. A: I might visit you this evening. B: Ok but don't come too late. We _____ dinner at nine o'clock.

4. A: Can you help me move some furniture tomorrow afternoon? B: No, sorry. I_____ then.

5. ___you _____football on the weekend?

6. What time will you be here tomorrow? Well, we are getting the 8:00 o'clock train so we _____ about 9:15.

7. ___ you still _____ at the factory next year?

8. I _____ when you get up. Don't wake me up!

9. They _____ coats now. It's much too hot.

10. She _____us tonight. She is just too busy.

# The Future Continuous: Exercise 2

Choose the correct tense: future simple or future continuous. The first one has been done for you.

1. You don't need to do anything for dinner. I'll *be cooking* / <u>*cook*</u> it.

2. I think he *'ll be waiting / wait* for us already. We are a little late.

3. Don't ring too late or I'll *sleep / be sleeping*.

4. I can't wait for the weekend. This time tomorrow I'll *fly / be flying* to Italy.

5. We will *do / be doing* a test in class tomorrow at 6:00 so I need to prepare tonight.

6. When we arrive in England I think it will *rain / be* raining.

7. A: Do you want to go to a bar tonight? B: Sure, I'll *meet / be meeting* you at 7:00 o'clock at The Beer Garden.

8. A: Can you pick up Joel from school at 4:00 o'clock. B: No, I can't. I'll *drive / be driving* to the airport to collect my parents.

9. Do you think it will *rain / be raining* much this winter?

10. Hurry up, I'll *be / be being* an old man by the time you're finished!

# The Future Continuous: Exercise 3

Complete the following sentences in either the future continuous or future simple using one of the verbs below. The first one has been done for you.

**Get sleep do run come make do study help travel**

1. I <u>will get</u> you a cup of tea. You look exhausted.

2. Why don't you come to visit me on the weekend? I won't _____ anything important.

3. Well I usually go to bed at 10:00 o'clock so if you call after that I _____.

4. This time next year I _____ my own company.

5. _____ they _____ us a cup of tea when we visit do you think?

6. Mike will be late home tomorrow. He _____ home by bus.

7. Sorry, I can't get there before 9:00. I _____ by car and the roads are really congested at that time.

8. _____ you _____ me carry this, please?

9. _____ you _____ at this Uni next year, or are you transferring?

10. Tarquin, have you fixed the computer. No, sorry. I _____ it tomorrow.

# The Future Perfect: Structure and Use

**Structure:** subject + will + have + past participle

**Examples:** "He will have finished by the time I get there" "We will have been married for 6 years this June."

We form questions by inverting the subject and "will" and form negatives by replacing "will" with "won't."

**Examples:** "Will you have finished the book before the holiday is over?" "They won't have thought of that."

We use the future perfect in two ways:

1. To talk about an action that finishes before a certain time in the future. For example, "The game will have finished by 8:00" (We don't know exactly when the game finishes but it is some time before 8:00) or "They will have finished all the food before we get there. (Again we don't know exactly when they will finish the food but it will be before we arrive. No food for us!)

2. To talk about a state that continues up to a point in the future and that may continue beyond this point. For example, "I will have been a doctor for 12 years next Christmas" (So a state, being a doctor, that continues until a point in the future, Christmas, and seems likely to continue beyond that) or "They will have lived in Peru for 8 years when we visit them in November." (So again, a state, living in Peru, that continues up to a point in the future, November, and maybe beyond.)

# The Future Perfect: Exercise 1

Choose the correct tense: future perfect or future simple. The first one has been done for you.

1. When you come home next month we will *be / <u>have been</u>* engaged for 2 years.

2. I will *become / have become* a historian when I finish University.

3. Did you break it? Oh, no. She will *be / have been* angry when she sees that.

4. I'm selling the house next year. It's very sad as it will *be / have been* in our family for 203 years when we finally let it go.

5. When the movie finishes we will *go / have gone* home.

6. We're late. They will probably *start / have started* without us.

7. I will *live / have lived* with my mum and Dad for 6 years this June. I should really move out.

8. A: Is Simon still upset? B: Yes, but I think he will *calm / have calmed* down by tonight.

9. A: Are we going to the beach this weekend? No, it will *be / have been* too cold.

10. A: Are you coming? B: Yep, hang on, I will *finish / have finished* in a few minutes.

# The Future Perfect: Exercise 2

Complete the following future simple or future perfect sentences using a verb in below. The first one has been done for you.

**visit clean  go get (x2) decide make bite eat**

1. I don't think there will be any food left when we get there. They <u>will have eaten</u> it. (eat)

2. A: Can you buy some bread? B: Sure, I _____ some when I go out later (get)

3. We _____ pizza for 3 days in a row if we have one today! (have)

4. We _____ what do when we get there and see what it's like. There's no point thinking about it now. (decide)

5. Mike _____ every country in Europe when he gets back from Italy. (visit)

6. Geoff and Maggie are working today. They _____ 20 bikes for their customers by the end of the day. (clean)

7. That dog _____ him if it gets angry. (bite)

8. When they arrive we _____ them a nice cup of tea. (make)

9. I _____ watched every episode of this TV show if I don't miss the one tomorrow. (watch)

10. I _____ when you get back so you will have to make yourself something. (eat)

63

# The Future Perfect: Exercise 3

Complete the sentences with the words in brackets. One will be in the future simple, and the other in the future perfect. The first one has been done for you.

1. I wonder why he's not here yet. We<u>'ll be</u> (be) late if he doesn't hurry up and all the best stuff <u>will have gone.</u> (go)

2. A: Are Rita and Marcia coming to our house again? They _____ (be) here every night this week. When ____ they _____ us a rest? (give)

3. I _____ (finish) this book by tomorrow then I _____ (lend) it to you.

4. One day the sun _____ (stop) shining. Hopefully, humans _____ (move) to another planet before that!

5. I hope this movie _____ (get) more interesting or we _____ (waste) 2 hours.

6. She _____ (live) with us for 20 years next month. I think I _____ ask her to move out!

7. We _____ (be) married for 10 yrs. I think I _____ (buy) a very special anniversary gift.

8. I ____ (clear up) so that we _____ (finish) before we want to go to bed.

9. I'm looking forwards to the play tonight. I think it ____ (be) good. We _____ (see) every Shakespeare play after this one!

10. I think John _____ (finish) work by now. Oh yes, that's the door. I ____ (get) it.

# The Future Perfect Continuous: Structure and Use

**Structure:** Subject + will + have + been + present participle

**Examples:** "I will have been studying for 5 years next June" "She will have been running for two hours"

We form questions by inverting the subject and "will" and negatives by replacing "will" with "won't."

**Examples:** "Will they have been thinking about it?" "I won't have been walking"

We use this tense in a similar way to the future perfect tense, to indicate that an action or state will continue up to (and maybe beyond) a specific time in the future. We almost always say the duration of the activity or state with this tense. For example, "I will have been running for 6 hours by ten o'clock" (I love running! I started or will start running at four o'clock, will be running at ten o'clock and, who knows, may continue running after ten o'clock) or, "They will have been living here for 6 years soon."

It differs to the future perfect tense in that there is often more emphasis on the continuous nature of the verb rather than a result. Compare, for example, "I will have eaten the cake" and I will have been eating the cake for 10 minutes." In the first example the cake is finished, in the second it is probably not. Or compare, "She'll have read the book" to "She will have been reading the book." In the first example, the book is finished, in the second, probably not.

# The Future Perfect Continuous: Exercise 1

Choose the correct tense: future perfect, future continuous or future perfect continuous. The first one has been done for you.

1. I will have <u>watched</u> / been watching all the Bond movies when this one finishes.

2. She will have *fished / been fishing* for five hours soon. I hope she catches something soon!

3. We will have *gotten / been getting* home by then.

4. I will *have worked / been working* on this for six months soon. And it's still not finished!

5. They will have *finished / been finishing* their home work by 6:00.

6. They will have *eaten / been eating* for 2 hours when Tracey arrives. They sure are hungry.

7. I will *be drinking / have been drinking* cocktails on the beach at this time tomorrow.

8. In five minutes, when little David gets out of class, I will *be waiting / have been waiting* for two hours.

9. By the time we finish we will *be / have been* studying the whole day.

10. A: Are you free for lunch later? B: No, sorry I'll *be working / have been working* through my lunch hour today.

# The Future Perfect Continuous: Exercise 2

Complete the following future perfect continuous sentences using one of the verbs below. The first one has been done for you.

Swim run work (x2) paint look watch try study smoke

1. I'll have been swimming for 5 hours soon. No wonder I'm tired!

2. We _____ every day for 5 months soon. I feel quite healthy.

3. When he graduates, he _____ for 5 years.

4. In 6 years I _____ for 40 years. I have to give up!

5. Look, we _____ T.V for 5 hours soon. Let's go for a walk instead.

6. Elizabeth _____ for the same company for 2 years soon. A new record for her.

7. Tom and Mary _____ for a new house for a whole year soon.

8. Can you make me some sandwiches before you leave John. I'll have them for lunch. I _____ all morning and will be too tired to make them myself.

9. By 3:00 we _____ the house for 6 hours. I think we can take a break then as we will be almost finished.

10. I _____ to get her to marry me for an entire year this Monday.

# The Future Perfect Continuous: Exercise 3

Complete the following sentences in either the future perfect continuous or future continuous using one of the verbs below. The first one has been done for you.

**think live look wait move go use argue play listen**

1. I will have been living here for 6 years soon. The time passed very quickly.

2. They _____ after Ringo the dog for 1 month when we collect him.

3. Mike's sister _____ the computer all day soon. I wish she'd let me have a go

4. Johnny and I _____ to Mexico next month.

5. Tina _____ for us in the restaurant unless we are late.

6. Janice and her friends _____ about the bill for 2 hrs soon.

7. We _____ to the bar soon. Are you coming?

8. Come on, we're late. By the time we get there the movie _____ for over half an hour.

9. I _____ to my brother's baby screaming all day so I should buy some earplugs!

10. Yes, I can give it to him. I _____ him tonight.

# Answer Key

## The Present Simple: Exercise 1

1. reads

2. collect

3. loves

4. go

5. go

6. annoy

7. bites

8. studies

9. goes

10. hates

## The Present Simple: Exercise 2

1. do you get up

2. does Maria get home

3. don't like

4. do they attend

5. Does John like

6. do you like

7. doesn't rise

8. Do they take

9. Why does he smoke

10. don't drink

## The Present Simple: Exercise 3

1. eat

2. do...live

3. takes

4. don't come

5. is

6. does...cost

7. costs

8. goes

9. doesn't go

10. Do...exercise

## The Present Continuous: Exercise 1

1. am watching

2. am doing

3. is playing

4. am trying

5. am working

6. are meeting

7. is studying

8. is having

9. are having

10. is barking

## The Present Continuous: Exercise 2

1. are you doing

2. am not going

3. Are they coming

4. are you doing

5. Is he using

6. are not swimming

7. is not doing

8. is not working

9. are not going

10 is not working

## The Present Continuous: Exercise 3

1. am not swimming

2. is drinking

3. Are you going

4. are you eating

5. am not sleeping

6. is cycling

7. are decorating

8. Are you hiding

9. are not

10. Are you moving

# The Present Continuous vs. the Present Simple: Exercise 1

1. I'm watching

2. are you doing

3. boils

4. I'm not working

5. are playing

6. I want

7. Do you understand

8. always drink

9. I don't like

10. I sleep in

# The Present Continuous vs. the Present Simple: Exercise 2

1. is reading

2. don't eat

3. smells

4. am working

5. don't drink

6. am going

7. drive

8. are going

9. isn't joining

10. don't believe

# The Present Continuous vs. the Present Simple: Exercise 3

1. damages

2. don't read

3. Does taste

4. come

5. is happening

6. costs

7. live

8. don't chase

9. am dripping

10. Are…going

## The Past Simple: Exercise 1

1. walked

2. was

3. loved

4. collected

5. caught

6. watched

7. scored

8. ate

9. stayed

10. slept

## The Past Simple: Exercise 2

1. I didn't go

2. did you do…stayed

3. Did you ask...nobody told

4. Did you borrow…did you leave

5. Did John mention

6. you remembered…I didn't forget

7. I broke it

8. I didn't do

9. I saw…They looked

10. they tell…it sounded

## The Past Simple: Exercise 3

1. didn't go

2. went…enjoyed…was

3. used

4. was…couldn't

5. didn't sleep…was

6. did say…seemed

7. didn't do

8. passed

9. Did…see…had

10. fell…broke

# The Present Perfect: Exercise 1

1. have been

2. has worked

3. haven't seen

4. have found

5. Have…met

6. hasn't read

7. has had

8. haven't bought

9. has broken

10. haven't seen


# The Present Perfect: Exercise 2

1. have eaten

2. Has …painted

3. Have…finished

4. has…gone

5. haven't been

6. has been

7. Have…finished

8. have invited

9. Have…got

10. have been

## The Present Perfect: Exercise 3

1. for

2. since

3. for

4. since

5. since

6. for

7. since

8. for

9. since

10. since

# The Present Perfect vs. the Past Simple: Exercise 1

1. correct

2. incorrect

3. incorrect

4. incorrect

5. correct

6. incorrect

7. correct

8. correct

9. correct

10. correct

# The Present Perfect vs. the Past Simple: Exercise 2

1. went

2. did you see

3. I've broken

4. I've lived

5. Have you had

6. hasn't changed

7. Have you ever been

8. I've forgotten

9. I've forgotten

10. wrote

# The Present Perfect vs. the Past Simple: Exercise 3

1. lived

2. has lost

3. was

4. killed

5. loved

6. did…get

7. have…been

8. did…get

9. Have…walked

10. gained

## The Past Continuous: Exercise 1

1. was reading

2. were drinking

3. Were…cleaning

4. weren't wearing

5. was…doing

6. Were…feeling

7. was thinking

8. was cooking

9. was singing

10. weren't feeling

## The Past Continuous: Exercise 2

1. was walking

2. Did…see…watched

3. were arguing…arrived

4. did..crash…were…talking

5. Did…let ("was…letting" is also possible)…needed

6. lived

7. went

8. was playing…went

9. met…was shopping

10. wrote…died

## The Past Continuous: Exercise 3

1. was walking

2. talked

3. caught

4. went

5. drank

6. was sleeping

7. slept

8. was having

9. saw…was trying

10. were arguing

## The Present Perfect Continuous: Exercise 1

1. Have you been cooking

2. have…been living

3. have been smoking

4. has been driving

5. have…been doing

6. have been working

7. has…..been doing

8. Are…..using

9. have been thinking

10. have been waiting


## The Present Perfect Continuous: Exercise 2

1. have you had

2. been running

3. have eaten

4. been smoking

5. been working

6. been thinking

7. eaten

8. seen

9. been playing

10. caught

# The Present Perfect Continuous: Exercise 3

1. eaten

2. been doing

3. put

4. been running

5. been planning

6. been doing

7. finished

8. been learning

9. been drinking

10. been turning

## The Past Perfect: Exercise 1

1. had…been

2. had found

3. had got / gotten

4. had hurt

5. had forgotten

6. had…lived

7. had been

8. had left

9. hadn't eaten

10. had…had


## The Past Perfect: Exercise 2

1. had completed

2. Had…seen

3. hadn't thought

4. had stayed

5. had lost

6. had brought

7. Had…repaired

8. had…left

9. hadn't bought

10. had taken

## The Past Perfect: Exercise 3

1. took

2. went

3. hadn't been

4. had forgotten

5. had been

6. had learnt

7. married

8. caught

9. Did you hear

10. went

## The Past Perfect Continuous: Exercise 1

1. had been living

2. had been painting

3. had been walking

4. had been stealing

5. had…been sailing

6. had been thinking

7. had been cooking

8. had...been doing

9. had…been doing

10. had been taking

## The Past Perfect Continuous: Exercise 2

1. got…had been waiting

2. had been seeing…asked

3. moved…had been living

4. had been waiting…took

5. couldn't hear…had been listening

6. had been drinking…started

7. shot…had been killing

8. had been living…became

9. had been jogging…thought

10. wanted…had been working

# The Past Perfect Continuous: Exercise 3

1. had been raining

2. met

3. had been cleaning

4. didn't write

5. had been playing

6. was

7. drove

8. had been working

9. had been swimming

10. saw

## The Future Simple: Exercise 1

1. will be

2. will get

3. will live

4. will melt

5. will beat

6. will ask

7. will do

8. will run

9. will be

10. will meet

## The Future Simple: Exercise 2

1. Are you going to

2. will

3. am going to

4. will

5. am going to

6. will

7. will

8. is going to

9. Is he going to

10. will

## The Future Simple: Exercise 3

1. am going to be

2. will do

3. are…going to go

4. am going to make

5. will do

6. Are…going to go

7. will be

8. will be

9. will be

10. are going to move

## The Future Continuous: Exercise 1

1. will be feeling

2. will be staying

3. will be having

4. will be working (or sleeping, but that goes somewhere else!)

5. Will…be playing

6. will be arriving

7. Will…be working

8. will be sleeping

9. won't be selling

10. won't be meeting


## The Future Continuous: Exercise 2

1. cook

2. be waiting

3. be sleeping

4. be flying

5. be doing

6. be raining

7. meet

8. be driving

9. rain

10. be

## The Future Continuous: Exercise 3

1. will get

2. be doing

3. will be sleeping

4. will be running

5. Will…make

6. will be coming

7. will be travelling

8. Will…help

9. Will…be studying

10. will do

## The Future Perfect: Exercise 1

1. have been

2. become

3. be angry

4. have been

5. go

6. have started

7. have lived

8. have calmed

9. be

10. have finished


## The Future Perfect: Exercise 2

1. will have eaten

2. will get

3. will have had

4. will decide

5. will have visited

6. will have cleaned

7. will bite

8. will make

9. will have watched

10 will have eaten

## The Future Perfect: Exercise 3

1. will be....will have gone

2. will have been...will...give

3. will have finished...will lend

4. will stop...will have moved

5. will get...will have wasted

6. will have lived...will ask

7. will have been married...will buy

8. will clear up...will have finished

9. will be...will have seen

10. will have finished...will get

## The Future Perfect Continuous: Exercise 1

1. watched
2. been fishing
3. gotten (got)
4. been working
5. finished
6. been eating
7. be drinking
8. have been waiting
9. have been
10. be working

## The Future Perfect Continuous: Exercise 2

1. will have been swimming
2. will have been running
3. will have been studying
4. will have been smoking

5. will have been watching

6. will have been working

7. will have been looking

8. will have been working

9. will have been painting

10. will have been trying

## The Future Perfect Continuous: Exercise 3

1. will have been living here

2. will have been looking

3. will have been using

4. will be moving

5. will be waiting

6. will have been arguing

7. will be going

8. will have been playing

9. will be listening

10. will be seeing

# Appendix 1

## The Present Simple: "S" / "ES" / "IES"

When we use "he," "she," or "it" we add "s," "es" or "ies" to the verb. For example, "He eats" "She goes" or "It flies." This is the third person singular.

The rules are as follows:

Normal verbs: verb + "s." For example, "eats," "sees," "smokes" and so on.

Verbs that end with a consonant + "y": omit the "y" and add "ies." For example, "tries," "fries," "hurries" and so on.

Verbs that end with "ch" "sh" "o" "s" or "ss": verb + "es." For examples, "watches," "washes," "goes" and so on.

And that's it!

# Appendix 2

## The Present Participle

The spelling rules for forming the present participle are somewhat complex. However, here we go!

The rules are as follows:

Normal verbs: verb + "ing." For example, "waiting," "listening" "talking" and so on.

Verbs that end in a silent "e": omit "e" and add "ing." For example, "moving" "pacing" "racing" and so on.

Verb s of one syllable that end vowel consonant (but not x y z): double final consonant and add "ing." For example, "running," "patting," "putting" and so on.

Verbs of two syllables which stress the second syllable: double final syllable and add "ing." For example, "occurring," "preferring," regretting" and so on.

Verbs that end "ie": omit "ie" and add "ying." For example, "lying," "dying" and so on (there aren't many of these.)

Verbs that end "c": add "king." For example, "panicking," picnicking," "frolicking" and so on (there aren't many of these either.)

And that's it!

# Appendix 3

## Common Irregular Verbs

1. Be: am/is/are was/were been

2. Begin: begin began begun

3. Beat: beat beat beaten

3. Bite: bite bit bitten

4. Blow: blow blew blown

5. Break: break broke broken

6. Bring: bring brought brought

7. Buy: buy bought bought

8. Catch: catch caught caught

9. Choose: choose chose chosen

10. Come: come came come

11. Cost: cost cost cost

12. Cut: cost cut cut

13. Dig: dig dug dug

14. Do: do did done

15. Dream: dream dreamed/dreamt dreamed/dreamt

16. Drink: drink drank drunk

17. Drive: drive drove driven

18. Eat: eat ate eaten

19. Fall: fall fell fallen

20. Fight: fight fought fought

21. Find: find found found

22. Fly: fly flew flown

23. Forget: forget forgot forgotten

24. Forgive: forgive forgave forgiven

25. Get; get got got/gotten

26. Give: give gave given

27. Go: go went gone

28. Grow: grow grew grown

29. Hang: hanged/hung hanged/hung

30. Hide: hide hid hidden

31. Hurt: hurt hurt hurt

32. Know: know knew known

33. Leap: leap leaped leapt

34. Learn: learned/learnt learned/learnt

35. Lose: lost lost lost

36. Make: make made made

37. Meet: meet met met

38. Pay: pay paid paid

39. Prove: prove proved proven

40. Read: read read read

41. Ride: ride rode ridden

42. Ring: ring rang rung

43. Rise: rise rose risen

44. Run: run run run

45. Say: say said said

46. See: see saw seen

47. Shut: shut shut shut

48. Sing: sing sang sung

49. Sink: sink sank sunk

50. Sit: sit sat sat

51. Sleep: sleep slept slept

52. Smell: smelled/smelt smelled/smelt

53. Speak: speak spoke spoken

54. Spend: spend spent spent

55. Steal: steal stole stolen

56. Swear: swear swore sworn

57. Swim: swim swam swum

58. Stand: stand stood stood

59. Steal: steal stole stolen

60. Take: take took taken

61. Teach: teach taught taught

62. Tear: tear tore torn

63. Tell: tell told told

64. Throw: threw threw thrown

65. Understand: understand understood understood

66. Wake: wake woke woken

67. Wear: wear wore worn

68. Write: write wrote written

Printed in Great Britain
by Amazon